Also by Evelyn McFarlane & James Saywell

If . . . (Questions for the Game of Life)
If ^{2} . . . (500 New Questions for the Game of Life)

If[3] . . .

If³. . .

(Questions for the Game of Love)

Evelyn McFarlane & James Saywell
Illustrations by James Saywell

Villard/New York

All rights reserved under International and Pan-American Copyright
Conventions. Published in the United States by Villard Books, a
division of Random House, Inc., New York, and simultaneously in
Canada by Random House of Canada Limited, Toronto.

VILLARD BOOKS is a registered trademark of Random House, Inc.

Library of Congress Cataloging-in-Publication Data is available.

ISBN: 0-679-45637-6

Random House website address: http://www.randomhouse.com/

Printed in the United States of America on acid-free paper

98765432

First Edition

The authors would like to dedicate this book
to all those who have given them love,
and who have received theirs.

If[3]...

Love. Romance. Sex.

From the imaginative lover to the imaginary one, our *imaginations* play a central role in our love lives. Pity the person who believes there exists no connection between the heart and the imagination, or pity their lover, anyway. From the first time we begin to discover there's a thing called love—tumultuous, chaotic, confusing, frightfully powerful, and stunningly joyous—we begin to imagine what might be if . . .

And as long as we are able to love (in other words, as long as we are alive), our imaginations help us through it, fill in the gaps, make us hopeful, steel our nerves, augment our romantic ideas, protect our humility, guide our actions, and help keep things interesting. Would we dare enter into love otherwise?

Yet as wonderful and wrenching as romantic love can be, it remains startlingly incomprehensible, and the mysteries of our own hearts tantalize us. Can we know more? Are we meant to? Ask yourself some of these questions, and ask those you love, or would like to. Where will they take you? What will they reveal? Do you have the courage to answer? Be prepared for anything.

And always, always, treasure the game of love.

We would like to add that some of the following questions are rather direct, and personal, and not everyone will choose to ponder them, but in no case do we intend offense.

If you were to complete the phrase "A life without love . . . ," how would you finish it?

If you had to have sex simultaneously with two people you know, who would you want them to be?

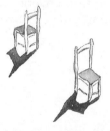

If you could have anyone in the world say one romantic thing to you, what would it be, and who would utter it?

If you could make love one more time with someone from your past, who would you choose?

If you had to watch your lover or spouse have sex with someone else, but could determine who it would be, who would you choose?

⚜

If you could personally undress anyone you know that you have never seen naked, who would you disrobe?

⚜

If you could kiss—but only kiss—one person you know anytime you wanted, who would it be?

⚜

If you had to name the most sensual part of your own body, what would you pick?

If you wanted to nonverbally signal to your lover in public that you wanted to make love, how would you do it?

If you could have a sensuous massage every day from someone famous, who would you choose?

If you could grab the buttocks of someone famous, whose would you grab?

If you wanted to turn your lover on as quickly as possible, what means would you use?

If you had to repeat the sexiest words anyone has ever said to you, what would they be?

If you were to identify the biggest turn-off in sex, what would you say it was?

If you went back in time to have sex with someone from your high school that you didn't have sex with then, who would you pick?

If from now on you could only have sex at a certain time of the day, when would it be?

8

If you were to have oral sex with someone famous right now, who would it be?

━·━ ≣◆≣ ━·━

If you could receive a sexual proposition from any one person, who would it be, and how would you want them to do it?

━·━ ≣◆≣ ━·━

If you were to name the most romantic thing you've ever done for someone else, what would it be?

If you were to define "kinky," how would you do it?

If you had to select the sexiest word in the English language, what would you say it is?

—————✠—————

If you had to involve (directly) one type of food in your next sexual act, what would it be?

If you had to pick the person with the hottest body you know but have never slept with, who would you say has it?

—————✠—————

If you could change one thing about the way your lover makes love, what would it be?

If you could try one thing in bed that you've never done, what would it be?

If you had to choose the person with the most remarkable sexual reputation of anyone you've known, who would win?

If you were to pick the worst misogynist you know, who would you say it is?

If you had to name the most extreme man-hater you know, who would it be?

If you had to name the most erotic book you have ever read, what would you pick?

If you had to describe the sexiest dream you've ever had, which one would qualify?

If you could have lost your virginity to someone you have met since, who would it be?

If you were to name the sexiest part of your mate's body, what would it be?

If you had to name the noisiest person you have ever had sex with, who would it be?

⊷ ▰◈▰ ⊶

If you were to name the one part of your body you most like to touch, what would it be?

⊷ ▰◈▰ ⊶

If you were to describe the kinkiest thing you would do under the right circumstances, what would it be?

⊷ ▰◈▰ ⊶

If you were to name the person you've made love with who was the biggest surprise (for better or for worse) in bed, who would you say it was?

13

If you had to name the biggest turn-on you have experienced in the history of your sex life, what would it be?

If you were to name the most romantic moment in your life so far, what would you say?

If you were to recall the most humorous thing that has happened to you in bed, what would it be?

If you could have changed one thing about the first time you had sex, what would you alter?

If you were to name a person whose attraction toward you is incomprehensible, who would it be?

If you were to think of a couple you know about whom you would say, "What on earth is he doing with her [or she with him]?," who would it be?

If you were to think of a famous couple about whom you would say, "What on earth are they doing together?," who would it be?

If there was one moment in the history of your love life when you were truly scared of the situation you were in, when would it be?

If you had to pick your best masturbation fantasy, what would it involve?

If you had to choose the best music to make love to, what would you pick?

If, for the rest of your life, you could achieve an instant orgasm by being touched on one particular spot on your body, where would you want it to be?

If you could be amazing at only one specific thing in bed, what would you want it to be?

If you had to hear one barnyard sound every time you had an orgasm, what would it be?

If you could change one thing about your lover's private parts, what would you change?

If you had to smell one food every time you had sex, for the rest of your life, what would it be?

If you could have any opera singer personally sing you a romantic aria, who would it be, and what would they sing?

17

If you could have changed one thing about your most recent sexual experience, what would it be?

If you had to name your favorite place to masturbate, where would it be?

If you were to repeat the most romantic thing anyone has written to you in a letter, what would it be, and by whom?

If you had to pick the most romantic moment in any film from history, what would you say?

If you had to name the "dirtiest" thing you have ever done, what would qualify?

If you could have your lover experience one thing you do that they now can't, what would it be?

If you could have videotaped any sexual experience you've ever had, which would you choose to record?

If you were to name the person who lost their virginity at the youngest age you know, who would it be?

If you were to repeat the funniest nicknames you have ever heard for each of the private parts, what would they be?

If you were to talk about the greatest lips you have ever kissed, how would you describe them?

If you were to name the best place that you ever made love, where would you say it was?

If you could have changed one thing about your own wedding ceremony, what would be revised?

If you were to decorate one room (secretly if you prefer) in your house, solely devoted to your erotic life, what would you put in it?

If you were to name the sexiest hotel room you have ever stayed in, which would you pick?

If you were to pick the most romantic city or foreign country you know, which would win?

If you were going to elope tonight, where would you go?

If you had to recall the riskiest place you've ever had sex, where would it be?

If you were to select the moment in your life when you looked the sexiest, when would it be?

If you were to pick a moment when your mate looked the sexiest they ever have, when would it be?

If you were to name the woman you know who has most enjoyed her pregnancy, who would it be?

If you were to pick the best and worst wedding presents you got, what would they be, and from whom?

If you had to describe the most erotic thing men can wear, what would you say?

If you could "unknow" any sexual fact, what would you choose?

If you had to have one television show on while you were making love, which one would you want?

23

If you had to pick the best advice that someone gave you at, or about, your own wedding, what was it, and who said it?

━━━✦━━━

If you had to confess the dirtiest thing you've ever done in the dark of a movie theater, what would you say?

━━━✦━━━

If you could have sex in any single make of automobile, which would you choose?

━━━✦━━━

If you had to name the dumbest place you've ever had sex, where would it be?

24

If you had to have one part of your anatomy dyed permanently blue, what part would you pick?

If you were to choose the person you find quite sexy despite being otherwise unattractive, who would you pick?

·—· ≍◆≍ ·—·

If you had to name the one person who most truly tested your sexual self-restraint, who would it be?

·—· ≍◆≍ ·—·

If you could do one physical thing to your lover while they slept, without them knowing about it at the time, what would you do?

If you had to have given any one person a sexual affliction, who would you have given it to, and what would it be?

If you could have a photo of any one moment from your wedding that was not recorded, what would it be of?

If you could invite a celebrity to join you in a threesome, who would you want?

If you could give back one thing a lover gave you, what would it be?

If you could lose your virginity over again to someone famous, who would you want it to be?

⊶ ≡◈≡ ⊷

If you had to pick the two people you would least like to watch having sex together who currently do, who would they be?

If you were to make love in a public place, where would it be?

⊶ ≡◈≡ ⊷

If you were to have any author write a novel about your love life, who would you have do it?

27

If you could plan your ideal honeymoon, what would it entail?

***

If you could have any single view from your bed, what would it be?

If you could pick the last person you will ever make love to, who would you select?

***

If you could invent a new method of birth control, what would it be like?

If you could go back and give one thing to a past lover, who would you choose, and what would you give?

If you could take back one thing you ever said in a romantic situation, what would it be?

If you could have made one person fall in love with you, who would you pick?

If you could have someone you know fall in love with someone else, who would they be?

29

If you could change the sexual practices of anyone you know, who would it be, and how would you change them?

If you could change one tradition regarding marriage, what would it be?

If you had to name the one thing you wear that makes you look sexy, what would you say it is?

If you were to hire an escort tonight, what type of person would you request, and what services would you ask for?

If you had to be the mattress of one famous person, whose would you want to be?

＋＋ ≡◈≡ ＋＋

If you were to carry with you at all times a plaster cast of one part of your lover's face or body, what part would it be?

＋＋ ≡◈≡ ＋＋

If you could temporarily freeze the world and everyone in it (except yourself), what sexual things would you do, and to whom?

＋＋ ≡◈≡ ＋＋

If you were planning your wedding now and could hold it any-where you wanted, where would you have it?

If you had to describe the kinkiest thing you've ever done, what would you say?

If you could go back and change one thing about your wedding night after the guests were all gone, what would you alter?

If your best friends were to hire an escort for you without warning you beforehand, what qualities do you think they would request?

If you were to plan your version of the perfect pre-wedding party (stag/bachelorette) for your next wedding, what would be included?

If you had to have one of your friends always give you the intimate details of their love life, who would you wish it to be?

If you could go back and say one thing to someone you were infatuated with in school, what would you say, and to whom?

If you were to name the person you most regret ever having kissed, who would get the prize?

If you could hear the unedited fantasies of anyone you know, whose would you want to listen to?

If you could hear the romantic fantasies of anyone famous, who would you select?

If you could reach any part of your own body to kiss that you can't now, what would it be?

If you could change the sexual attitudes of anyone you know, who would it be?

If you were to photograph yourself in a sexy pose, what pose would you strike?

If you had to give the age of the youngest person you've ever slept with, what would it be?

If you had to give the age of the oldest person you've ever slept with, what would it be?

If you had to pick the age of the youngest and oldest people you *would* ever sleep with, how old would they be?

If you were to name the part of other people's bodies you most like to touch, what would it be?

If you had to use one household substance as a sexual lubricant (that you have never before used), what would you try?

If you could have known one thing about your spouse on your wedding day that you have learned since, what would it be?

If you had to pick one friend to plan your stag or bachelorette party, who would you want to do it?

If you were to name the company that has the most sensual advertisements, who would win?

If you were to confess the most embarrassing moment in your sexual history, what would it be?

If you had to pick the closest you have ever come to being caught in the act, when would it be?

If you were to pick the greatest single day in your sexual history, what would it be?

If you were to name the most erotic person you see regularly that you know you will never sleep with, who would it be?

If you had to name the nationality who make the best lovers, in your own experience, what would you say?

＊＋ ≍◆≍ ＋＊

If you could have your lover say one thing to you more often than they do (and mean it), what would you want to hear?

＊＋ ≍◆≍ ＋＊

If you could have returned the love of someone you rejected in the past, who would it be?

＊＋ ≍◆≍ ＋＊

If you had to put a new sexually explicit tattoo on your body, where would you have it located, and what would it be?

If every time you had sex a big bell would chime somewhere in the world, where would you want it to be?

If everyone in the world had to donate one dollar to charity every time they had sex, how long do you think it would take to wipe out poverty?

If you could have said one thing during your wedding ceremony that you didn't, what would it be?

If you were to recall the dumbest thing you said at your wedding, what would it be?

If there was one spot on your lover's body that had to be put permanently off-limits to your touch, where would you want it to be?

If every man on Earth had to have genitals identical to those of someone you have known, whose would you pick?

If you had to name one thing ever said to you by a lover that you wish hadn't been, what would it be?

If you were to recall the strangest physical thing you've ever had happen during lovemaking, how would you describe it?

If, for the rest of your life, you had to always eat the same meal right before you had sex, what would you want it to include?

If you were to pick the sexiest advertisement of all time, which would you say it was?

If you could have freckles on one part of your body that you don't, where would they be?

If you could remove one birthmark or scar from your body, which would it be?

If you could have any poet from history write a love poem to you, who would you pick?

If you were to choose the best meal to be eaten right after making love, what would it be?

If you could have invited anyone you didn't to your own wedding, who would it be?

If you could have *not* invited anyone you had to (and did) to your own wedding, who would it be?

If you had to pick your best "making-up" after a lovers' quarrel, when would it be?

If you had to recall the person who was the most difficult to face the morning after, who would it be?

If you had to pick the person you've known or met who, with charisma alone, could have seduced you, who would it be?

If you had to choose your own sexiest characteristic, what would it be?

If your mate were to give you a new tattoo while you were sleeping, where would they most likely place it, and what would it be of?

—————

If you had to pick the one person in your life you have felt the strongest platonic love for, aside from members of your family, who would you say it was?

—————

If you could plan your own fiftieth wedding anniversary, what would it be like?

—————

If you were to name the two people you know who come closest to being soul mates, who would they be?

44

If you were to win an award for the time you made the most noise during sex, what occasion would be cited, and who were you with at the time?

If you could have objected at any wedding and put a halt to it, whose would it have been?

If you were to put one spot of your body off-limits to your lover's touch, where would it be?

If your lover could do one thing to you while you slept, without waking you up, what do you think they'd do?

If you could convert one heterosexual to homosexuality, who would you choose, and would it be temporary or permanent?

———— ⁛ ————

If you could convert one homosexual to heterosexuality, who would it be, and would it be for a day or a lifetime?

———— ⁛ ————

If you were to ask someone you love for a single proof of their love for you, what would you demand?

———— ⁛ ————

If you were to pick the most beautiful wedding ceremony you've ever been to, whose would you say it was?

If the feelings you experience in your genitals during orgasm could be replicated in one other part of your body every time you did one nonsexual thing, where would you want to feel it, and during what activity?

If you had to remember every person you've ever had sex with, how accurate could you be?

If you were to give a prize for the silliest name for sexual intercourse, what would win?

If you could only make love in one position for the rest of your life, which position would you want it to be?

If you could have had anyone from history show up at your wedding, who would you have wanted it to be?

—————◆—————

If you had to name the most beautiful wedding dress you've ever seen, whose would it be?

—————◆—————

If you were to describe the most romantic letter or note you have ever written, what would you say?

—————◆—————

If you were to name one spot on your body where you always like to be touched, what would it be?

48

If you were to pick the sexiest season for clothes, what would it be?

If any person you chose in the world accepted your offer of payment to watch them having sex, who would it be, and what's the most you would pay them?

If your lover asked you to do one thing (of your choice) that you've never done before, in order to prove your love for them, what would you do?

If you were asked to add one phrase or statement to all marriage ceremonies, what would you add?

If you had to name the two people you know who should most be a couple but aren't, who would you pick?

If you had to name the one spouse or mate of a friend you have most lusted after, who would it be?

If you could try one sexual position you never have, which one would it be?

If you could receive a love letter from anyone alive, who would it be from?

If you had to pick the worst quarrel you have ever had with a lover, what was it about, and who was it with?

If you were to devise a test to determine whether people were true soul mates, what would it entail?

If you could write (or rewrite) a prenuptial agreement for your own marriage, what would it say?

If you were asked to state at what age a person is ready to have sexual intercourse, how would you answer?

If you were now given ten dollars for every time you had masturbated in your life until the present, how radically would you be able to upgrade your standard of living?

If you could have attended any famous couple's wedding, whose would you choose?

If you were to demand one thing from your next divorce (other than money or children), what would you ask for?

If you were to guess what the most popular sex toy is, what would you say?

If you had to have the voice of someone you know coaching you in a whisper every time you had sex for the rest of your life, whose voice would you want it to be?

If you could see one romantic film again, which would it be?

<hr>

If the genitals of the entire opposite sex were to have the aroma of one food item, what would you pick?

<hr>

If you had to guess the average age that people today lose their virginity, what would you say?

If you could send a love letter to anyone alive and know that they would receive and read it, who would it be addressed to?

If you had to name the most romantic gift you have ever given, what would it be?

If you had to describe the best romantic gift you have ever received, what would it be, and from whom?

If you could write something to one of your lovers that would be opened and read by them only after you die, who would it be to, and what would it say?

If you could teach your children one moral lesson about love, what would it be?

If you were to name the one person you know who is lacking sound judgment about their own relationship, who would it be?

If you could eliminate one marital problem for everyone on Earth, what would you choose?

If you were to name the greatest regret of your romantic life, what would it be?

If you were to name the person you have known with the shallowest definition of love, who would you pick, and how would they define it?

—————— ❈✦❈ ——————

If you were to name the person you know who has been married the most often, who would it be?

—————— ❈✦❈ ——————

If you could ensure one thing about your children's love life, what would it be?

—————— ❈✦❈ ——————

If you had to name the best wedding gift you've ever heard of (besides money), what would it be?

56

If you could have one domestic chore also be an erotic act, which would you choose?

If you had to name the person you had your biggest childhood or adolescent crush on, who would it be?

＋＋ ＝◆＝ ＋＋

If you had to name the person you know that you'd least like to sleep with right now, who would it be?

＋＋ ＝◆＝ ＋＋

If you had to say how many times you've had sex, what would be your best guess?

If you were to pick the person who had the easiest pregnancy, who would it be?

If you were to pick the person who had the most difficult pregnancy, who would it be?

If you were to name the TV show with the most sexual imagery ever, which would it be?

If you could find out something about your lover's sex life before you knew them, what would you ask about?

If you were to pick the sport that develops the sexiest body type, which would it be?

If you were to select the most sensual dancer you have had the pleasure of dancing with, who would you pick?

If you were to name a person who you think needs to "come out of the closet," who would it be?

If you were to make your most seductive face, what would you look like?

If you were to select the most romantic book ever written, which would it be?

If you were to name the sexiest actor and actress ever, who would you choose?

If you had to name the least sexy actor and actress ever, who would it be?

If you had to repeat the most ridiculous thing you have ever uttered during sex, what was it, and who were you with?

If you were to name a place you would like to make love in that you haven't, what would it be?

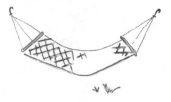

If you were to rate your love life as it is right now, on a scale from 1 to 10, what number would you choose?

— ≍✦≍ —

If you were to select the most romantic restaurant you know, which would qualify?

— ≍✦≍ —

If you were to describe the best thing any lover can do in the morning, what would it entail?

If you were to articulate the biggest difference between the way a woman loves a man and the way a man loves a woman, what would you say?

If you found your true love, how long would you *truly* wait for them to return your love?

If you were to name the one thing about your love life that you are most ashamed of, what would you say?

If you were to name a person in your life who you were attracted to but should not have been for some reason, who would it be, and why?

If you were to name the person you know with the most exaggerated opinion of their own attractiveness, who would you say it is?

⋯⋯ ⊨✦⊨ ⋯⋯

If you were to remember one romantic experience that changed your life, what would you say?

⋯⋯ ⊨✦⊨ ⋯⋯

If you were to choose the one thing that most convinced you that the person you are with is the right person to be with, what would you say?

⋯⋯ ⊨✦⊨ ⋯⋯

If you were to name the one thing that in the past gave you the strength to leave a lover, what would you say?

If you were to name the one romantic lover in your life that you have shed the most tears over, who would it be?

⊷ ⊰✦⊱ ⊶

If you were to name the two people you know who took the longest time to break up, who would they be?

⊷ ⊰✦⊱ ⊶

If you could shave anyone's entire body, whose would you pick?

⊷ ⊰✦⊱ ⊶

If you could have your body shaved by anyone, who would you want to do it?

If you were to choose the one material object that could best express or represent love, what would it be?

If you were to choose the most sensual room you have ever been in, what space would you pick?

If you were to choose the one type of women's makeup that is the best turn-on, what would you select?

If you were to choose the best wedding cake you have ever tasted, at whose wedding was it served?

If you were to name one person (more than any other) who you now cannot believe you were ever attracted to, who would it be?

+ ≖✦≖ +

If you were to name one person in your life who you will never have the right opportunity to say "I love you" to, who would it most likely be?

+ ≖✦≖ +

If you were to select the person you know who has broken the most hearts, who would you say it is?

+ ≖✦≖ +

If you were to name a person whose heart you truly broke, who would it be?

66

If you were to name the most bizarre fetish of anyone you know, what is it, and who has it?

If you were to name the most surprising place you have heard that someone you know has had sex, what would you say?

If you were to define the perfect marriage in a few simple sentences, how would you do it?

If you were to define the perfect divorce, what would you say?

If you had to name the man who has impregnated the most women, who would you guess it to be?

———— ✠ ————

If you were to recall your longest climax ever, how long did it last, and how did it come about?

If you were to say what the best thing about starting a new relationship is, what would it be?

———— ✠ ————

If you wanted to be aroused over the telephone by someone other than your current lover, who would be best at it?

If you were to plan a romantic evening that did not include sex, what would it be like?

If you were to continue the quotation "How do I love thee? Let me count the ways . . . ," what would "the ways" be for you in your current relationship?

If you could eliminate one emotion that has to do with romance, what would you get rid of?

If you were to name a person that you believe has never experienced true love, who would it be?

If you were to set regulations for pornography on the Internet, what would you propose?

If you could have anything occur on every wedding anniversary, what would you want to happen?

If you could pass one new national law related to sex, what would you ask for?

If you were to remember the quickest quickie you have ever had, just how quick was it?

If you were to choose the most difficult thing about ending a relationship, what would it be?

If you could give your kids one piece of advice about marriage that they would follow, what would you say?

If you could find out any single sexual statistic, what would you want to know?

If you could have found out something about sex sooner than you did, what would it be?

71

If you were to make one change to your home to improve your love life, what would you alter?

If you were to name an actor that others find sexy but you just don't, who would it be?

⊹ ≡◈≡ ⊹

If you could hire an escort for a friend, who would it be for, and what services would you order for them?

⊹ ≡◈≡ ⊹

If you had to name the person you know who is most afraid of romantic love, who would you say it is?

If you were to name the most insulting thing ever said to you by a lover, what would it be?

If you could give a prize for lovemaking to one person you have known, who would win it, and what would the prize be?

If you had to pick the most clever thing you've ever done in revenge, what would win?

If you had to accompany one couple you know on their honeymoon, who would you join?

If you were to prescribe the best cure for lovesickness, what would it be?

If you had to come up with just one word to describe each of your past lovers, what would it be?

If you had to choose a meal that best represented your love life, what would be on the menu, and where would you eat it?

If you were to recall one specific period of your life when you masturbated the most, when would it be?

If you had to pick the person it was the most difficult to break up with, who would it be?

If you were to name the two people who took the longest to finally commit to each other, who would they be?

If you had to say one thing you told somebody about your love life that you now wish you hadn't, what would it be?

If you were to name one person you had enormous luck in seducing, who would it be?

If you were to use a metaphor right now to sum up your love life, what would you say?

＋＋ ⪌◊⪋ ＋＋

If you could buy any sex toy for yourself, what would it be, what would you name it, and how much would you pay for it?

＋＋ ⪌◊⪋ ＋＋

If you could make love only one day of the year, which day would you choose?

＋＋ ⪌◊⪋ ＋＋

If you could forget one year of your romantic life, which one would you erase from your memory?

If you were to invent a replacement for the tradition of the wedding ring, what would it be?

If you were to guess the thing that would most surprise you about your parents' sex lives, what would it be?

If you were to describe the single most kinky thing you think your mate would do, what would you say?

If you had to name the most humiliating moment you have had involving a lover, what would you say?

If you were to pick the lover you have had who had the most beautiful sexual organ, who would win?

If you were to guess which of your lovers had the highest sperm count, who would it be?

If all of your ex-lovers were to say the same romantic thing about you, what would you prefer it to be?

If you had to confess one thing about your love life to your mother, what would you say to her?

If you could meet with one lover from your past right now to see how they are, who would you want it to be?

⊶—⊨◈⊨—⊷

If you were to pick a food that is the most sensual while being eaten, what would it be, and who would you love to watch eating it?

If you could have known everything one former lover did while out of your sight, which person would you pick?

⊶—⊨◈⊨—⊷

If you had to see, for the rest of your life, an image of someone you've known, while you are having sex, whose face would it be?

If you were to name a person you would like to watch while they are masturbating, who would you pick?

——— ≡✦≡ ———

If you were to state the longest length of time that lust for one single person can sustain itself, how long would you say it is, and under what conditions?

——— ≡✦≡ ———

If you were to remember the shortest romance you have ever had, which would it be?

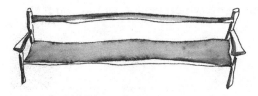

If you were to decide the best place to make love other than a bed, what would you say?

If you were to describe the saddest love story between two people that you know personally, what would you say?

If you were to name the most difficult "I love you" that you ever had to say, who did you say it to, and why was it so difficult?

If you were to name the situation where you had to fight the hardest to keep a person at bay, what would it be?

If you had to admit to one time when you were overcome with sheer animalistic lust for someone, what would you say?

If all of your children, gathered together, told you that they were gay, what would your reaction be?

━━━ ≡◆≡ ━━━

If your daughter told you she was pregnant and didn't know who the father was, what advice would you give her?

━━━ ≡◆≡ ━━━

If you had to name both the hardest and easiest people to give affection to that you know, who would they be?

━━━ ≡◆≡ ━━━

If you had to name the type of weather you find the most romantic, what would you say?

If you had to name the cutest romantic habit your lover has, what would you say?

If you had to name the most lethargic person in bed you ever knew, who would it be?

If you had to name the one thing you most fear about relation-ships, what would it be?

If you had to pick one smell you most readily associate with sex, what would it be?

If you could leave just one photograph of you and your spouse (that you already have) for the rest of your family to have forevermore, which one would it be?

❈

If you had to name the one incident that truly made you question your love for your mate, what would it be?

❈

If you were to think of the biggest misconception about marriage, what would it be?

❈

If you were forced to choose one thing more important in life than love, what would you pick?

If every time you masturbated in the next year you had to be observed by one person you know platonically, who would you pick?

⊶ ≍◆≍ ⊷

If you had to imitate the strangest sound anyone ever made while making love, what sound would you make?

⊶ ≍◆≍ ⊷

If one food for you could be an aphrodisiac, which food would you select?

If you were to identify a true symptom of lovesickness, what would you say it is?

If you had to name a person you know about whom you would say, "They are very sexy for their age," who would it be?

If you had to name the person who makes really great sounds during lovemaking, who would it be?

If you were to pick the relationship in which you faked more orgasms than any other, which would it be?

If you had to name the person you've never had to fake an orgasm with, who would it be?

If you had to guess the person you work with who is most likely to wear sexy underwear, who would it be?

If you had to name the one part of the human body—besides the sexual organs—that you consistently find sexy, what part would it be?

If you were to imagine one thing your lover could confess to you that would make you extremely upset, what would it be?

If you had to guess which of your friends' children will grow up to be the sexiest looking, who would you choose?

If you had to guess which person, among all those you know, is the kinkiest in private, who would it be?

If you had to guess who, among the people you know, would be the most disappointing in bed, who would be the one?

If you had to pick, from all the cars you've owned, the best one to make out in, which would it be?

If you had to admit to the raunchiest thing you have ever done in your parents' car, what would it be?

If you had to guess which of your friends' kids will grow up with the best attitude toward sex, who would you pick?

⚊⚌✦⚌⚊

If you had to rearrange all the sexual parts of your body, where would you put them?

⚊⚌✦⚌⚊

If you had to have the sexual organs of someone you know, whose would you take?

⚊⚌✦⚌⚊

If you had to name the least restrained person you have ever been to bed with, who would it be?

If you were to have a secret affair in your hometown or city, which hotel would you pick for your rendezvous?

If you had to name the most romantic singer in musical history, who would you pick?

⊷ ⊷

If you were to name a specific period of your life when you were the horniest, when would it be?

⊷ ⊷

If you had to name the most consistently sexy dresser of anyone you know, who would you choose?

If you had to name one thing you would find most difficult to forgive in your lover, what would it be?

If you were to name a celebrity who is extremely sexy and romantic for their age, who would you pick?

If you had to name the one person you would be most upset by finding out your lover had slept with, who would it be?

If you knew your lover was cheating on you, who is the one person you would be least upset about it being with?

If you had to name the person you know who could do much more with their looks or sex appeal, who would it be?

If you had to name the one lover you've had with a specific sexual specialty or talent, but who was not necessarily great in bed otherwise, who would it be?

If you could treat each of your parents to a romantic night with anyone in the world, other than each other, who would you pair them with?

If you had to name the biggest prude you've ever known, who would it be?

If you had to pick the person you think is sexier than everyone seems to realize, who would it be?

If you had to say what's both great and awful about making out in a car, what would it be?

If you had to name the delivery or repair person you'd most like to fool around with, who would you pick?

If you were to name a person who is truly beautiful in all ways, who would you pick?

If you had to name the one thing you least expected to be turned on by but then were, what would it be?

If you had to name the person who is most comfortable with their own sexuality, who would it be?

If you had to name the person who is least comfortable with their own sexuality, who would you pick?

If you could arrange a romantic weekend fling for two people you know who aren't a couple and never will be, who would you pair together, and where would they go?

If you had to name a situation where you have used your sensuality to get something other than sex, what would it be?

If you were to use one object every time you masturbated for the rest of your life, what would it be?

If you had to name the most physically demanding lover you ever had, who would it be?

If you were to define "sin" as it relates to sex, what would you say?

If you could have one of your sexual fantasies come true tomorrow, what would it be, and how would you prepare for it?

If you had to name the one place (besides bed) that you have masturbated most, where would it be?

If you had to choose the smell you most automatically associate with your lover, what would it be?

If you had to name the most disgusting thing your lover does, what would it be?

If you were offered a part in a hard-core porn film, how much money (minimum) would you do it for?

If you could improve your sex life in one way, how would you do it?

If you had to name the dumbest article on love or sex in a magazine that you have read, what would it be?

If you had to name the best advice you've ever heard a sex expert give, what would it be?

If you were to name the most surprisingly romantic thing your mate does, what would you say it was?

If you had to name the most difficult good-bye you ever said, what would it be?

If one of your grown children told you they had acted in a hard-core pornographic video for money, how would you react?

If your mate suddenly revealed to you that they were now attracted to your opposite sex, what would you say?

If you found out that your favorite political figure had acted in a hard-core porn film when they were very young, how would it affect your opinion or support of them?

If you had to name the one aspect of your own sexuality that you least understand, what would it be?

If you had to name the one lesson of love that took you the longest to learn, what would it be, and why?

If you had to name the most unusual relationship you know of, whose would it be?

99

If you had to have the birthmark of someone you know, whose would you pick?

If you were to describe the perfect amount and form of physical affection you would want every day, what would you say?

If you had to name the one part of your body that you would least want touched by someone you don't like, what would it be?

If you were to choose the most sensual music video you've ever seen, which would you pick?

If you could take revenge on any lover from your past, who would it be, and what would you do?

If you could bring one romantic literary character to life and meet them, who would you pick?

If you could go to bed with one person but always wake up with another (of the people you know), who would they be?

If you could guarantee that you will keep one sexual quality (e.g., technique, desire, physical trait) until you die, what would you want it to be?

If you were to buy your lover a sex toy for Christmas, what would you purchase?

—————— ✠ ——————

If you were to write an ad to put in the personals for a weekend fling, how would you word it?

—————— ✠ ——————

If you were to read a personal ad for a weekend fling that had the most chance of tempting you, what would it say?

—————— ✠ ——————

If you could have a platonic nap every day with someone, who would it be with?

If you were to pick the moment at which you were the most jealous, when would it be?

If you could make an improvement to condoms in any way, what would you change?

If you were to name the part of your body you would least like to have pierced, what would it be?

If you were to have a phrase tattooed on your lover's privates, what would it say?

If you were to name a person who you believe must be the most satisfied with their sex life, who would you pick?

If your lover's sexual organ were shaped in the form of a building, which structure would you prefer?

If you could rent a billboard to say something about love, what would you write, and where would you want it placed?

If you could make a miniseries about your love life, what would you title it?

If you were to name the person you had the most orgasms with in a single session of lovemaking, who would win?

If you had to wear one article of clothing you already own every time you went out on a date in the future, what would you select?

If you wanted to revive a flagging physical relationship, how would you go about it?

If you had to name the biggest sexual braggart you've ever known, who would it be?

If your lover could lose one inhibition, what would you want it to be?

⊷⊶ ⋈⊹⋈ ⊷⊶

If you could be bolder in one area of your love life, what would you pick?

⊷⊶ ⋈⊹⋈ ⊷⊶

If one physical part of you could be bigger, what would it be?

If one physical part of you could be smaller, what would you choose?

If you could create a bouquet of flowers for your loved one, what would it be made up of?

—⊷ ⟨⟡⟩ ⊶—

If your naked body were to be lathered with a certain kind of dessert, what would it be?

—⊷ ⟨⟡⟩ ⊶—

If you were to direct an erotic love scene for a film, what would it include?

—⊷ ⟨⟡⟩ ⊶—

If you could lose one inhibition, which would you choose?

If you could give someone a hickey in any shape and size, who would receive it, and on what part of the body?

If you were to give a new permanent body marking to your lover, what would it be, and where?

If at the height of passion your lover were to whisper or yell something, what would you want it to be?

If someone were to seduce you in a foreign language, which would you choose?

If you had to name the smallest space you've ever had sex in, where was it?

If you had to name a really naughty thing you've done at someone else's wedding, what would it be?

✦

If you had to pick the nationality of people that you find the most attractive, which would it be?

✦

If you could have one thing installed beside your bed, what would you want?

If you could have one part of your body glow in the dark, what part would it be?

——— ✠ ———

If your lover were to leave you now, what one thing would you want them to leave behind for you to remember them by?

If you could do one great trick with your tongue that you can't now do, what would it be?

——— ✠ ———

If you could determine the size and shape of your lover's sexual organs, what would they be?

If you had to name the most erotic piece of artwork you've ever seen, what would you choose?

If you had to name the one thing that should turn you on in bed but just never does, what would it be?

If you were to describe the one natural setting you'd most like to make love in, what would it be like?

If you could have only one sexual fantasy—repeatedly—for the rest of your life, what would it involve?

If you had to choose a foreign accent that you find sexy, what would you say?

If you had to name the worst thing you ever said to a lover in a heated moment, what was it?

If you were to name the people you know who have been married the longest, who would they be?

If you were to name the person you know who was married for the shortest time, who would win?

If you could learn one thing about your parents' honeymoon, what would you want to know?

If you had to recall your very first sexual thought, what would you say it was?

If you were caught by your children in bed having sex, what would you say (in one sentence)?

If you were to name the most sensual perfume on the market, which scent would win?

If you had to name the person who has the worst taste in girl-friends or boyfriends, who would it be?

If you were to recall the most romantic evening you have had that did not involve sex, what would it be?

If you could have anyone you know tuck you into bed every night with a single kiss, who would you pick?

If you could teach your kids one thing about romance, what would you tell them?

If you were to kiss the toes of anyone in the world, whose would you choose?

⋯ ⚊✦⚊ ⋯

If you had to include one animal in your next lovemaking, what kind would it be?

⋯ ⚊✦⚊ ⋯

If you had to name the person who has been most deceived by their mate, who would you select?

⋯ ⚊✦⚊ ⋯

If you could interview any porn star, who would you pick, and what would your first question be?

If you could have an existing law related to sex eliminated, what would it be?

◆

If you were to describe the sexiest bathing suit you've seen, what would you say?

◆

If you had to say one word every time you had an orgasm, what word would you pick?

◆

If you had to describe the intimate details of each of your sexual encounters to one person you know platonically, who would you pick?

If you were to be sent to a prostitute who had been already paid, what would you do with them?

———— ≍✦≍ ————

If you were to pick the least sexy fashion trend of your lifetime, what would it be?

———— ≍✦≍ ————

If you were to pick the period with the sexiest fashions during your lifetime, what would win?

If for the rest of your life you could have a single thing delivered to your bed right after you had sex (besides money), what would you want it to be?

If you had to pick the most affectionate type of animal, what would it be?

If you could have been the mistress or lover of any great figure from history, who would you pick?

If you were to have an orgy with any six people you know, who would you invite?

If you had to make love listening to the same piece of music for the rest of your life, what would you select?

If you could have stood up one person you should have, who would it be?

If you were to name the language that sounds the most romantic, which would it be?

If you could go back and change one thing about your honeymoon, what would it be?

If you were to name the best speech or toast you have heard at someone's wedding, who gave it, and what did they say?

If you were trying to be a matchmaker for two people you know, how would you do it?

⊷ ▬◈▬ ↢

If you could have only one person say "I love you" to you, who would you want it to be?

⊷ ▬◈▬ ↢

If you were to describe your overall sex life (from your first experience through your most recent), what would you say?

⊷ ▬◈▬ ↢

If you were to name a place where you would like to masturbate that you never have, what would it be?

120

If you could rewrite your marriage vows, how would you change them?

If you were to advise someone on the perfect way to elope, what would you say?

If you were to name the one thing that makes you feel sexy, what would it be?

If you were to come up with one positive result of a mate cheating on their spouse, what would it be?

If you had to name one sexual thing you pray that your lover will never ask you to do, what would it be?

If you could have any sculpture come alive to make love to, which piece would you want?

If there was one thing relating to your love life that you could be blackmailed for, what would it be?

If you were to dedicate any single thing to someone to show your love for them, what would it be, and to whom?

If you were to have a baby with someone with whom you could never have a relationship, whose child would you want?

If you could have sex with one pagan god, which would it be?

· · ⚌ ◆ ⚌ · ·

If you could produce a film about safe sex for kids, what would it be like?

· · ⚌ ◆ ⚌ · ·

If you had to pick a book title that most accurately sums up your love life, what would it be?

If you were to recall the time when you ruined the most clothes during the heat of passion, when would you say it was?

If you could meet the love of your life, where would you want the meeting to take place?

If you were the opposite sex for a year, what one sexual thing would you never do with a lover?

If you were to have a dead loved one as an inanimate object in your house, what would they be?

If you found out that your mate had once acted in a hard-core pornographic film, what would you do or say to them (and would you want to see it)?

If you had to name the most beautiful or impressive wedding or engagement ring you have ever seen, whose would it be?

If you could give one piece of sexual advice to the opposite gender, what would it be?

If you could give one piece of sexual advice to your own gender, what would it be?

If you had to recall the most shocking thing you have accidently seen going on between two people, what would it be?

If you could dedicate one work of art to someone you love, which would it be, and to whom would you dedicate it?

If you were to die for someone for the sake of love, who would you die for?

If you had to identify the darkest fictional character that you find erotic and sensual, who would it be?

126

If you could learn one dance to turn your lover on, what would you pick?

If you could only kiss your lover on one spot of their body forevermore, what spot would you choose?

If you could give Dr. Ruth one piece of sexual advice, what would you say?

If you could make love with your current lover, and include one lover from your past in the fun, who would you pick?

If you were to name a nonsexual thing that always arouses you, what would it be?

———◆———

If you were to recite any poem to your present lover, which would you choose?

———◆———

If you wanted to get the love of your life to fall in love with you, to what extremes would you go?

———◆———

If you found out the love of your life had only one month to live, how would you spend your time with them?

If you could say "I love you" only one more time, who would you say it to?

—————

If you could send your parents on a second honeymoon anywhere in the world, all expenses paid, where would you like it to be?

—————

If you had to make love under a giant photograph of one member of your family, who would you want it to be, and who wouldn't you want it to be?

If you had to define "love" in a few simple words, how would you do it?

If you have an interesting or humorous question or answer to contribute to sequels of *If . . .*, we would love to hear from you. Please send your response or new question to the address below. Please give us your name and age, and sign and date your contribution. Thank you.

Evelyn McFarlane
James Saywell
c/o Villard Books
201 East 50th Street
New York, NY 10022

E-mail:author@ifbooks.com
Website:http://www.ifbooks.com

About the Authors

Evelyn McFarlane was born in Brooklyn and grew up in San Diego. She received a degree in architecture from Cornell University and has worked in New York and Boston. She is now living in Florence, Italy, and spends her time painting and writing.

James Saywell was born in Canada. He studied architecture in Toronto and at Princeton. He designs buildings and furniture, paints, writes, and teaches architecture, and divides his time between the United States and Italy.